Play Like A Girl

by

Adriane Costa

Published in the USA by:
Adriane Costa

Printed in the United States of America
ISBN   978-1-7323726-0-3 (hardcover)
978-1-7323726-1-0 (paperback)

Book & cover layout by Darlene Swanson • www.van-garde.com

For Hannah,
and every girl wanting
to try something new

author, age 13

Preface

This photography project began as a way to show my five year old daughter that 'playing like a girl' is not an insult. I wanted to show her that girls can do anything they want and be just as successful and accomplished in it as a boy can.

Growing up as an athlete was never a question of if, but what. My parents always presented me and my sister with a variety of activities to choose from and supported every interest we had. Between my sister and myself we tried soccer, ballet, tap dancing, volleyball, gymnastics, swimming, ice skating, diving, softball, swimming, and water polo.

It never crossed my mind that I couldn't participate in any activity I wanted to. And I certainly wasn't self-conscious about how I ran or what I looked like while I was doing the sport.

So hearing my daughter question herself and what she may look like while being active shook me to my core.

I am 'mom-tographer;' a typical, suburban mom who also happens to really enjoy taking photographs and turned this passion into a business.

Before starting this series I had no sports photography experience, mostly focusing on portraiture. But through this project I have found I am drawn to the focus and precision that occurs when the body is captured in movement. Most of these girls are friend's daughters, neighbors, babysitters and other connections from throughout my community. I'm in awe of what each of these female athletes are capable of doing and how hard they work to be successful in their activity.

I want to share their beauty, determination, strength of character and achievements with the rest of our community and beyond.

Introduction

Each of the girls photographed in this book exemplify what it means to be strong, confident, fierce and empowered. Whether I knew them personally or met them through the reach of this project, they all left me in awe of their skill, dedication, and passion they put forth.

Although this series features girls from my small community, it is only the tip of the iceberg. In every town, city and state, there are hundreds of girls learning, practicing, completing and excelling in a huge variety of sports and activities.

After photographing each of them, I had the opportunity to ask them candidly why they did their sport and what it means to play like a girl. Their answers blew me away and made me swell with pride. Their words gave me chills and I knew that I had to somehow share this message with girls everywhere.

It makes me so proud to be raising a daughter in a community that supports our young girls to pursue any activity they chose. I hope these images can be shared with girls of all ages as an example to motivate them to follow their hearts and show what it really means to play like a girl.

"There is no limit to what we, as women, can accomplish."

Michelle Obama

I enjoy kickboxing because I like to spar.
It makes me feel powerful to kick. I also like building
muscle and feeling more confident. Kickboxing gave
me the confidence to stand up for myself and others.

I don't like that 'play like a girl' is used to say that
something is done badly or isn't good enough.
This motivates me to work harder and fight smarter.
Girls can be tough and strong. They may do things
differently than boys but that doesn't mean it is less.
I want to be one of the reasons playing like a girl
is the best compliment, even for a boy.

Raina, 11

I feel good when I'm playing basketball
because I am able to play and work well
with some of my closest friends.

To play like a girl means to
play with heart and hustle.

Mele, 15

I play basketball because my older brother always used to play. That's how I got into the sport and I've loved it ever since.

Playing like a girl means to play your heart out no matter the level of competition.

Lesila, 16

I love all parts of cheer; stunting, tumbling,
jumping and dancing. It makes me
feel cheerful and I have fun.
That's what play like a girl means to me,
to have fun and play my sport hard.

Hannah, 9

Play like a girl means to play your hardest,
every step, every throw, every movement
has a purpose. It doesn't matter if you win or lose,
but it matters that you played your hardest.

Sami, 17

To play like a girl may seem like a mean name,
a negative thought, but I think of it as a compliment
because it really is! To play like a girl means that
you are strong and are like no other.
To play like a girl brings out the true you.
Some people may think girls are not strong
but I always remember this: I am a girl,
I am strong, and I am myself.

Anna, 9

I really enjoy practicing gymnastics.
I always like to be at the gym.
I like flipping and doing tricks.
Play like a girl means I am strong
as any boy in my sport.

Sophia, 10

I do gymnastics because I love the reward
of competing and being able to show off
all the hard work I've put in!

Play like a girl to me means that just
because we are the "weaker" sex
it doesn't hold us back from excellence
in physical activities like gymnastics.

Kelley, 18

Play like a girl means to you can be
your own person and have your
own personalities and be
who you are meant to be.

Emma, 9

I love to be around animals.

The fact that I get to ride them is incredible.

When I am riding I feel like I am flying; it is amazing!

Gianna, 11

I've been so thankful to grow up in an era
where girls have similar opportunities to excel
in sports as boys do. Playing like a girl doesn't
mean playing weak or playing fearful.
It means playing with the best of your ability,
as would anyone else. It means fearlessness,
strength, and resilience. Its no coincidence that
some of the best female role models have
also been athletes at some point in their lives.
Playing like a girl transcends the boundary
between athletics and any other form of work,
teaching us to be better people because of it.

Lexi, 16

Kung Fu has helped me develop my mind,
body and spirit unlike any other activity I have ever done.
Through kung Fu I have formed long lasting friendships
with my peers and teachers at kung Fu; these friendships
are different from any others I have.

Kung Fu has helped me to feel confident and
break out of my shell more to reach my full
potential as an individual.

Play like a girl means a lot of things.
It means not holding back, putting everything
you can into it, proving to yourself what you are
capable of, and to be focused, fierce,
passionate, and strong.

Rebecca, 13

Sofia, 13

Play like a girl means that even the
smallest girl can have
the biggest heart

Kennedy, 10

When I swim, I feel strong!
Someday I want to be
in the Olympics.

Madison, 7

Girls can do anything,
and be as strong or
stronger than a boy.

Abby, 9

'Play like a girl' means putting forward
everything you've got and
not just being somewhere
because you have to.

Olivia, 14

Playing like a girl is not different
than playing like a boy.
We both have the same goal
in the game; to play my hardest
and try to win.

Cali, 11

Playing like a girl is
doing what you love
and doing it as
aggressively as you can.

Alissa, 13

Play like a girl means that I can play rough
or I can play with a doll;
it means I can do whatever
I want, it doesn't matter.

Eme, 9

I train and compete in
Olympic weightlifting
because I love it.
When I lift I feel amazing!

Elle, 12

Running makes me feel very happy.
Running like a girl means being strong
and never giving up

McKenzie, 6

Gymnastics makes me feel good about myself.
Playing like a girl means to be yourself and
you can be stronger than a boy.

Samara, 10

I play softball, tennis and skateboard.

I thought skateboarding looked fun and wanted to try it.

The best is going down hills on my board.

When I hear 'play like a girl' from a boy

it makes me want to show them

I can skateboard better than they can.

Kathryn, 10

I play sports because its fun.
When I play soccer I feel happy.

Taylor, 10

Try your best and never
let anyone stop you!

Riann, 12

I play softball because it
is challenging and fun!

Ava, 10

It makes me so angry when people use
'play like a girl' in a negative and demeaning way.
Play like a girl means strength and I am a
strong supporter of girl power.

Gracie, 16

When I play tennis
I feel happy and strong!

Piper, 9

I play volleyball because I really enjoy the sport.
When I play, I try to be the best I can be.

Grace, 13

One of the best feelings is knowing
you played your hardest.

Play like a girl means to play my sport
as well as I can, as hard as I can, and to not give up.
Even when playing the hardest competition,
to keep going and encourage my teammates.

Natalie, 14

I love to express myself through dance.
It makes me feel powerful and graceful at the same time.
Dancers need to be strong but make it look effortless.

Try your best and prove that girls are just as
strong or even stronger than boys.
Be fierce because there are no limits.

Stephanie, 12

CPSIA information can be obtained
at www.ICGtesting.com
Printed in the USA
BVHW02*1106280718
522537BV00003B/3/P